LOST TEMPLE OF THE AZTECS

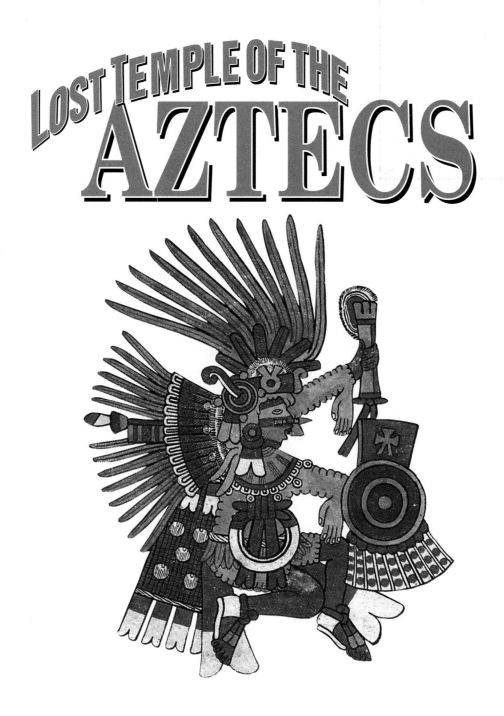

First published in the United States by
Hyperion Books for Children
a division of the Walt Disney Company
114 Fifth Avenue
New York, NY 10011-5690

First Edition
3 5 7 9 10 8 6 4 2

Library of Congress Cataloging-in-Publication Data

Tanaka, Shelley.
The lost temple of the Aztecs: what it was like when the Spaniards invaded Mexico/by Shelley Tanaka;
illustrations by Greg Ruhl.
p.   cm.
"A Hyperion/Madison Press book."
Summary: Uses the discovery of the temple in Mexico City, what was the Aztec city of Tenochtitlan,
to introduce the story of the Spanish conquest of Moctezuma and his empire in the sixteenth century.
ISBN 0-7868-1542-6
1. Aztecs—History—Juvenile literature. 2. Aztecs—Social life and customs—Juvenile literature.
3. Mexico—Discovery and exploration—Spanish—Juvenile literature. 4. Mexico—History—Conquest,
1519-1540—Juvenile literature. [1. Aztecs—History. 2. Indians of Mexico—History. 3. Mexico—
History—Conquest, 1519-1540.] I. Ruhl, Greg, ill. II. Title.
F1219.73.T35 1998
972'.02—dc21

Madison Press Books
40 Madison Avenue
Toronto, Ontario
Canada M5R 2S1

Printed in Singapore

LOST TEMPLE OF THE AZTECS

What it was like when the Spaniards invaded Mexico

AN I WAS THERE BOOK

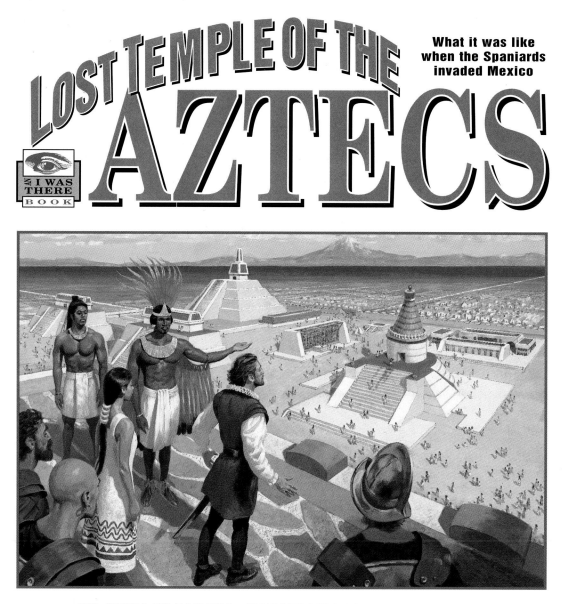

BY SHELLEY TANAKA, ILLUSTRATIONS BY GREG RUHL

Diagrams and maps by Jack McMaster, Historical consultation by Eduardo Matos Moctezuma

A HYPERION/MADISON PRESS BOOK

PROLOGUE

February 21, 1978

The *zocalo* was still dark. The trolley cars crossing the far corner of Mexico City's main square were not yet filled with people on their way to work. Between the cathedral and the presidential palace, workmen were digging ditches for electrical cables, anxious to beat the thick heat and pollution that would wrap around the city by midday.

Suddenly they struck something hard. It was a flat round stone covered with intricate, mysterious carvings.

A team of experts was called. They discovered that the giant disk, almost ten feet (three meters) in diameter, depicted Coyolxauhqui, the ancient moon

Professor Eduardo Matos Moctezuma, a descendant of Emperor Moctezuma, supervised the excavation of the Great Temple.

goddess. Further digging revealed that the stone lay at the foot of some buried steps. Beneath a block of stores and parking lots in the center of Mexico City, they had found the Great Temple of the Aztecs, the cornerstone of what was once the most powerful empire in North America.

Professor Eduardo Matos Moctezuma undertook the excavation. He knew that he was witnessing the discovery of a lifetime. A graduate of the Mexican National School of Anthropology, he had long experience in excavating Aztec sites. But his interest was more than professional. Through his mother's ancestors, his family tree led directly back to one of the most famous and tragic rulers in history.

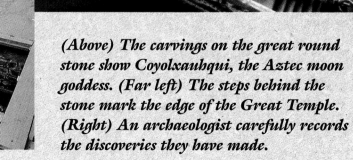

(Above) The carvings on the great round stone show Coyolxauhqui, the Aztec moon goddess. (Far left) The steps behind the stone mark the edge of the Great Temple. (Right) An archaeologist carefully records the discoveries they have made.

Long before the Europeans came to North America, a very different kind of metropolis stood on the spot where Mexico City is now. It was called Tenochtitlán, and it was the capital city of the Aztec empire.

Five hundred years ago, Tenochtitlán was a city of 250,000 people. It was built on an island in the middle of a sparkling blue lake. Canals crisscrossed the city between blocks of spotless white buildings and lush green gardens. Long causeways led to the mainland, where snowcapped mountains loomed in the distance.

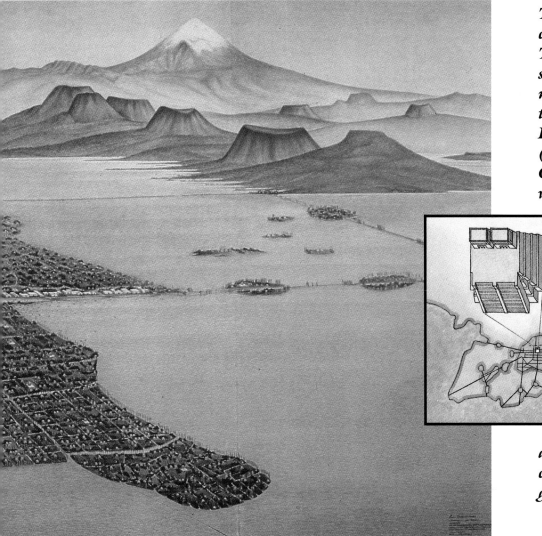

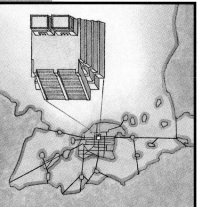

The Aztecs' capital, Tenochtitlán, stood in the middle of the shallow Lake Texcoco. (Below) The Great Temple was built

at the very center of the great city.

square surrounded by shrines and palaces. Its steep steps were stained with the blood of human sacrifices. This was where the Aztecs worshipped their gods, where their conquered enemies brought gifts and tributes, and where the Aztec ruler Moctezuma received important guests.

One fateful day in 1519, an unusual group of visitors approached Tenochtitlán. The Aztecs had never seen such people. Their skin was oddly white, their faces were covered with hair, and they wore metal clothing from head to foot. They came with strange, wild-eyed beasts, and they carried heavy weapons that clanked and gleamed in the sun.

Were they friends, or enemies? Should they be destroyed or treated as guests?

Moctezuma decided to welcome the strangers. After all, what could his mighty nation of warriors have to fear here, within the walls of their great city?

The first Europeans who saw Tenochtitlán found the city so beautiful, they thought it must be enchanted.

The Great Temple stood at the heart of this remarkable city. Nine stories high, it faced a huge

PART ONE

THE STRANGERS ARRIVE

April 1519

The ships came from the east. They just appeared on the horizon one day, as if they had dropped from the sky. They were bigger than any boats the people had ever seen, and they floated toward the shore like small mountains.

When Moctezuma's messengers saw the ships, they hurried back to Tenochtitlán.

"Strange people have come to the shores of the great sea," they told their ruler. "They have very light skin and long beards, and their hair only comes down

An illustration from a Spanish book of the time shows Cortés's expedition coming ashore near what is today the city of Veracruz, Mexico.

to their ears. They sit on huge deer that carry them wherever they want to go."

Moctezuma listened to the news in silence. His mind raced.

Quetzalcoatl has appeared! he thought. He has come back to reclaim his throne!

It was happening, just as the ancient prophecy had foretold. Long ago, according to legend, Quetzalcoatl, the great god of learning and creation, had sailed east on a raft of serpents to a mysterious land across the ocean. But he had promised to come back, and this was the predicted year of his return.

WHO WERE THE AZTECS?

By the time Cortés arrived in 1519, the Aztecs ruled a great empire in what is now Mexico (right). Originally from a land farther north called Aztlán, they arrived on the shores of Lake Texcoco in the fourteenth century. But the people living there wouldn't let them settle. So they created their city right in the lake, on rocky outcroppings and shallow marshes. (According to legend, the Aztecs' priests had a vision of an eagle eating a snake atop a cactus (left) and, where they saw the eagle, they built their capital. Today the eagle on a cactus is part of the Mexican flag.) The Aztecs traded with people around the lake, and grew richer. Later, they expanded, creating an empire by defeating their neighbors in war.

Tenochtitlán

Moctezuma knew there had already been signs that things were not well with the gods, that some momentous change was about to come to his people. Two years before, a great tongue of fire had streaked across the night sky, like a spear plunged into the very heart of the heavens. At dawn, the sun destroyed the fire, but the next night it appeared again. And so it went on for the better part of a year, and each night the people watched with terror. Would the sun, the source of all life, continue to destroy the fire? Might the sun one day stop rising?

There were other signs of death and ruin. Temples burst into flames. The great lake that surrounded Tenochtitlán swirled and bubbled up as if it were boiling with rage. The nights echoed with the sound of a woman wailing.

Moctezuma was filled with fear and confusion at these unnatural happenings. The gods must be looking unfavorably on the richest and most powerful empire in the land.

And now, it seemed, one of the gods had returned. Quetzalcoatl had arrived.

THE AZTEC YEAR

The Aztec calendar was shown as a round disk (left and inset), since the Aztecs saw time as being like a wheel, endlessly turning. Each day had a name (rain, crocodile, rabbit, and so forth) and a number from 1 to 13. Every 13 days a new month began, and there were 20 months in the Aztec year — which was only 260 days long. The Aztecs also had a 365-day calendar, which they used to keep track of their many religious ceremonies. Once every 52 years, the first day of the 260-day calendar and the first day of the 365-day calendar were the same. This marked the start of a new "century" or cycle, a very important time in the Aztec world. By coincidence, according to the Aztec calendar, the year Cortés landed happened to be the year given for the possible return of Quetzalcoatl.

11

Moctezuma gathered his chiefs around him. "Our lord, Quetzalcoatl, has arrived at last. Hurry to meet him. Tell him that his servant Moctezuma has sent you to welcome him back to his throne, and take him these gifts."

Moctezuma's messengers traveled to the coast. They placed their gifts in canoes and paddled out to where the huge ships floated offshore. The pale-skinned strangers let down a ladder, and the messengers climbed on board. They were taken to the leader, whom the strangers called Cortés. Surely he was Quetzalcoatl himself!

The messengers kissed the deck at Cortés's feet. "We bring these gifts from your servant Moctezuma," they told him. "He guards over your kingdom and keeps it safe for your return." Then they adorned

Among the priceless treasures Moctezuma sent to Cortés was this pendant of a two-headed snake. This would be worn suspended on a chain that went around the neck. The snake was a symbol of the god Quetzalcoatl.

Cortés with a serpent mask made of turquoise and a headdress of shimmering blue-green quetzal feathers. They draped gold and jade bands around his neck, arms, and legs. They placed a cape of ocelot skin and sandals of glistening black obsidian at his feet, along with all the other gifts — serpent-head staffs and spears inlaid with green jade, masks, shields, and fans heavy with gold and turquoise.

Cortés looked at everything they had given him. "Are these your gifts of welcome?" he asked. "Is this all you have brought?"

"Yes, lord," the messengers replied. "This is everything."

Cortés ordered his men to fasten irons around the messengers' ankles and necks. Then he fired a huge gun. The messengers had never seen such a

THE AZTECS AND THEIR GODS

I n the Aztec world, every aspect of life had a god who governed it; a god to be called on and praised but whose help could never be taken for granted. Among the most powerful gods was Tezcatlipoca, whose name meant "smoking mirror." This powerful deity was also referred to as "maker of himself" and "lord of the high and mighty." Other deities controlled specific parts of nature, such as Xipe Totec, the god for seeds, or Chalchiuhtlicue, (opposite top) also known as "she of the jade skirt." She was the goddess of springs, rivers, lakes, and the sea. There was even a god for chance and gambling, Xochipilli (opposite bottom).

Two other very important deities seem to have been living leaders who, over time, became revered as gods. Huitzilopochtli was the patron of war, and one of the two shrines on top of the Great Temple was dedicated to him. Quetzalcoatl (opposite), whose name meant "feathered serpent," had been worshipped long before the Aztecs ever arrived on the scene. Legend says that he had sailed away on a raft into the sunrise. When Cortés arrived, people believed that he might be Quetzalcoatl and that he had come back to claim his kingdom.

sight. They fainted from fear and fell to the deck.

The strangers revived them with wine and food.

"I have heard about your people," Cortés said. "They say that one Aztec warrior can overpower twenty men. I want to see how strong you are." He gave them leather shields and iron swords. "Tomorrow, at dawn, you will fight, and then we will find out the truth."

"But this is not the wish of our lord and your servant, Moctezuma," the messengers answered. "He has only told us to greet you and bring you gifts."

"You will do as I say," said Cortés. "Tomorrow morning we shall eat. After that you will prepare for combat."

Then Cortés released them. Moctezuma's messengers got back in their boats and paddled away as quickly as they could. Some even paddled with their hands. When they reached land they scarcely stopped to catch their breath before hurrying back to Tenochtitlán to tell Moctezuma about the terrifying things that had happened.

They described the strange sweet food they had eaten and the gun that had sounded to them like deafening thunder.

"A ball of stone comes out shooting sparks and raining fire. It makes smoke that smells of rotten mud. When the ball of stone hits a tree, the trunk splits into splinters, as if it has exploded from the inside.

"They cover their heads and bodies with metal. Their swords are metal, their bows are metal, their shields and spears are metal. Their deer carry them on their backs, making them as tall as the roof of a house."

When Moctezuma heard all this, he could not sleep or eat. He felt as if his heart had shriveled up inside him.

"What will happen to us now?" he asked. He ordered two captives to be sacrificed, and sprinkled the messengers with their blood. After all, they had completed a difficult mission. They had seen the face of Quetzalcoatl and had spoken with the god himself.

WHO WERE CORTÉS AND MOCTEZUMA?

ernan Cortés was a Spanish landowner who lived on the island of Cuba, which had been visited by Columbus in 1492 and then taken over by the Spanish. Like many men who had moved to the New World, Cortés dreamed of grasping a fortune for himself. With official backing from the governor of Cuba and using some of his own money, Cortés put together an expedition. The governor withdrew his official support, but Cortés left anyway, gambling on the success of his venture.

Moctezuma was the ninth Aztec emperor or *tlatoani*, an Aztec term that meant "speaker." He was the second ruler to bear the name Moctezuma. He had become emperor in 1502, picked, in the Aztec fashion, by the other nobles. Moctezuma was a little older than Cortés, thirty-eight to the Spaniard's thirty-three.

Moctezuma sent warriors to take food to the strangers. They also took captives to sacrifice so the gods could drink their blood. Only human blood, the most precious of all things, could keep the gods fed and satisfied. Without it, dreadful punishments could befall the people — earthquakes, floods, and hailstorms that destroyed their crops and brought hunger and starvation. Why else did the Aztec knights go to war, if not to capture victims who could be offered to the gods?

But when Moctezuma's warriors killed the captives in front of Cortés and his men and presented them with a dish of their blood, the strangers were appalled. They spat on the ground, and turned away in disgust. Moctezuma could not understand this.

What sort of gods were these who did not welcome human blood?

He sent his magicians to meet Cortés. Perhaps they could conjure up a great wind to blow him away, or at least make him turn back to where he had come from. But all their efforts were in vain.

"We are powerless against him," they told Moctezuma. "We are nothing compared to these strangers."

Moctezuma was very frightened. He wanted to run away, hide himself from the gods in a cave. His people heard of their ruler's despair. They whispered together when they met in the streets, as panic and uncertainty spread through the city. What terrible things, they wondered, lay ahead of them?

October 8, 1519

The strangers were coming to Tenochtitlán. And as they made their way inland, Moctezuma received puzzling and terrifying reports.

First Cortés and his men stopped in the land of Tlaxcala, home of the Aztecs' mortal enemies. The Tlaxcalans eagerly joined Cortés and swelled his ranks.

Next the strangers passed through Cholula, where there was a temple to Quetzalcoatl. But once there, they turned their guns on the Cholulans, shot them with crossbows, or speared them to death. Then they burned the temple and hurled the statues of

A TEAM PLAYER

Although the army that Cortés had with him was very small — just 600 Spaniards — it was powerful. Spanish soldiers had steel armor and helmets for protection, swords and crossbows, guns and horses. More important, they fought as an organized unit. Soldiers equipped with long spears could hold off the enemy. Other soldiers using guns and crossbows could break up an enemy charge. After that, soldiers on horses could charge their opponents, and send them fleeing.

Quetzalcoatl to the ground.

Moctezuma heard this news with cold fear. Why would a god destroy his own temple, kill his own priests?

Then his messengers described to him how Cortés had told the prince of a neighboring land about the Christian god. Cortés said he had been sent by the king of Spain to save the prince's soul, to make him a member of the one true faith. Cortés held up a cross, and the prince knelt down in front of it and allowed himself to be baptized and given a Spanish name.

When the prince told his mother what he had done, she called him a fool. She said he must have lost his mind to be won over so easily by a handful of barbarians like these Spaniards. Her son was angry. He threatened to cut off her head. And he told her she would be baptized, too, whether she was willing or not.

When Cortés was making his way through the mountain pass before entering the valley where Tenochtitlán lay, Moctezuma sent his nobles to meet him. This time they took many gifts of gold — necklaces and armbands and shields. The Spaniards' eyes lit up when they saw the gold. They pawed over it and fingered each piece like monkeys. They couldn't get enough of it. Now they were more eager than ever to reach Moctezuma and his city that held such riches.

Moctezuma gathered together his chiefs. Should they welcome the strangers or fight them? The Aztecs were the greatest warriors in the land. They had conquered their neighbors on every side. Surely they could defeat these Spaniards, too.

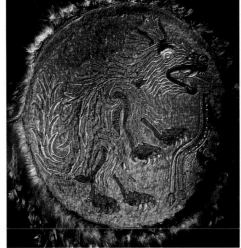

"Do not let these strangers into your house," warned one of Moctezuma's chiefs. "They will throw you out and by the time you try to recover what you have lost, it will be too late."

The others agreed, but Moctezuma refused to listen. He decided to welcome the Spaniards as friends.

Then he waited in silence. And all of Tenochtitlán waited with him.

A LONE WARRIOR

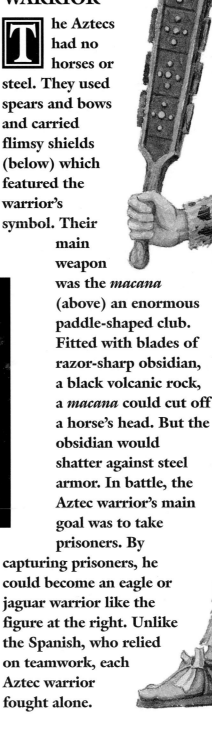

The Aztecs had no horses or steel. They used spears and bows and carried flimsy shields (below) which featured the warrior's symbol. Their main weapon was the *macana* (above) an enormous paddle-shaped club. Fitted with blades of razor-sharp obsidian, a black volcanic rock, a *macana* could cut off a horse's head. But the obsidian would shatter against steel armor. In battle, the Aztec warrior's main goal was to take prisoners. By capturing prisoners, he could become an eagle or jaguar warrior like the figure at the right. Unlike the Spanish, who relied on teamwork, each Aztec warrior fought alone.

PART TWO

FRIENDS OR FOES?

T he Spaniards covered the south shore of the lake. Then they began their march into Tenochtitlán.

They came like a dark serpent over the causeway leading to the island city. Their huge spotted dogs led the way, panting and sniffing, their tongues dangling. Then came a single man bearing a flag on his shoulders. As he walked, he waved the red and gold banner from side to side, making it billow and snap.

Behind him came four horsemen. They pulled their animals from side to side, waving their swords as if they were checking for danger. Then came men dressed for battle. They were covered in metal that glistened in the sun like running water. Their heavy swords rattled and clashed against their shields.

Soldiers on horseback came next. The horses bellowed and snorted and stirred up clouds of dust. Sweat and foam poured off their coats like soap suds. Their hooves on the ground sounded like the rain of heavy stones.

Behind the horses came a group of men bearing crossbows. As they walked they narrowed their eyes and sighted along their weapons, pointing at things and testing their aim. Their thick cotton armor reached down to their knees, and they had decorated their helmets with quetzal feathers. More horsemen and men with guns followed. From time to time they raised their weapons and fired them into the air, scattering shot and filling the sky with smoke and fumes.

And finally there was Cortés, gleaming like the sun, surrounded by his warriors and servants. Behind him walked the many native allies who had joined him, including a large number of Tlaxcalans. They were dressed for war, too, and as they entered the city of their Aztec enemies, they waved their spears and bows. Some dragged bundles of supplies and food. Others pulled huge guns mounted on wooden wheels.

Moctezuma went to meet the visitors, accompanied by a number of his chiefs. He was carried on a litter. His finest ruler's robes and headdress were embroidered and decorated with feathers. His sandals were heavy with gold. He presented the visitors with trays of sunflowers, jasmine, and magnolia flowers. He hung garlands and golden bands around their necks, placed wreaths on their heads, and draped chains of flowers on them.

At last, Cortés and Moctezuma stood face to face. To the right of Cortés stood a beautiful native woman who acted as interpreter for the two leaders. Her keen dark eyes

HOW DID CORTÉS TALK TO MOCTEZUMA?

Cortés spoke Spanish. Moctezuma spoke Nahuatl. When they first met, they could not talk directly. But Cortés had a Spaniard with him who knew Mayan. He in turn spoke to a young native woman known as Doña Marina or Malinché, from a people who lived near the Aztecs. She spoke Mayan and Nahuatl and, later, Spanish. But at first talks between Cortés and Moctezuma would have gone from Spanish to Mayan to Nahuatl and back again.

WHEN CORTÉS MET MOCTEZUMA

ortés and Moctezuma first met outside the center of Tenochtitlán, but for years no one knew exactly where. Then in the late 1960s, a construction crew for the Mexico City subway came across the ruins of a small temple (top), which experts believe to be the place of the fateful first meeting. Today, because Mexico City is many feet higher than Tenochtitlán, only the top of the temple is visible. (Above) It is now part of Pino Suárez subway station.

scanned the crowd as she spoke. She never left Cortés's side.

"So are you Moctezuma?" Cortés asked.

"Yes," Moctezuma replied, and he bowed. "You must be tired," he said. "I see you have finally come to claim your city, which I have been watching over for you. The ancient rulers have long said you would return across the sea one day. Now you are here. Please come to the palace and rest."

Cortés nodded. "We have waited a long time to meet you," he said. "Do not be frightened. We are your friends."

The Spaniards climbed down from their horses and gathered around Moctezuma. They clapped him on the back and clutched him by the shoulders.

Moctezuma's followers watched. They saw themselves surrounded by Tlaxcalans. They saw their most precious gifts draped on the bodies of men dressed in steel. They saw their ruler, whose face was usually hidden, being pawed and pushed by strangers.

And as the people watched, some of Moctezuma's chiefs turned from him and quietly slipped away.

November 12, 1519

Moctezuma led the Spaniards up to the flat roof of one of his temples. The city lay spread out on all sides. The temples and great squares glistened in the sunlight. Three wide stone causeways stretched across the water to the distant shores of the lake, while canoes brought goods and food as tribute from people whom the Aztecs had conquered.

Moctezuma pointed out the sights with pride. Workers plastered and painted the adobe homes of nobles and tended flower-lined courtyards and terraces. Peasants repaired their thatch-roofed huts made of reeds and mud. On the outskirts of the island, floating gardens of corn, beans, peppers, tomatoes, squash, and flowers were tended by farmers. They stood waist-deep in the canals that lined the fields and scooped up thick bottom mud to spread on the soil.

Below the temple Moctezuma's guests could see the market square. They heard the voices of thousands of people offering special meats for the table. There were turkeys, ducks, rabbits, and little hairless dogs. Merchants had their goods spread out in front of them on cloths — jewelry, medicine herbs, rope, fabric, deer and jaguar and otter pelts, sandals, feathers. There was no money, but everything could be traded.

The spotless city was filled with people.

Merchants carried their goods in large sacks on their backs. Nobles paraded about in their fur cloaks, jewels, and plumes. Warrior knights wore their eagle helmets and jaguar skins. Commoners moved through the streets dressed in simple loincloths and coarse cloaks. Everyone was in a hurry, like ants in a busy colony.

Moctezuma could tell the visitors were impressed. They looked around in all directions. Some pointed and exclaimed excitedly at what they saw. Others simply stared, as if in a dream.

When they walked through the ruler's private gardens and zoo, even Cortés gaped with wonder. The scent of rare flowers rose up around them. In the Palace of Birds, thousands of songbirds, parrots, great blue herons, hummingbirds, flamingos, birds of prey, and butterflies filled the air with their songs and wing beats. There were snarling wild cats, wolves, and foxes in cages, and hissing rattlesnakes in large pots.

But when Moctezuma showed the visitors the shrines of the Great Temple, Cortés and his men recoiled at the sight of the blood that stained the steps and sacrificial stones. They shrank from the priests, whose faces were painted black and whose hair and robes were crusty with dried blood. They covered their mouths and noses at the smell of the stone vessels where the hearts of victims were burned and offered to the gods.

Moctezuma could not understand their horror. To him the Great Temple was beautiful. Its walls were decorated with brilliant murals; its sculptures had been made by the finest craftsmen in the land. The temple was his people's pride, and the blood sacrifices were their tribute to the gods who allowed the city to run so smoothly.

In the 1930s, the famous Mexican painter Diego Rivera created a set of murals depicting Tenochtitlán. (Left) Rivera shows what an Aztec market looked like. As people barter for gourds and tortillas, Moctezuma (seated center) watches, holding a fan. (Above) Aztec nobles dressed in their finery.

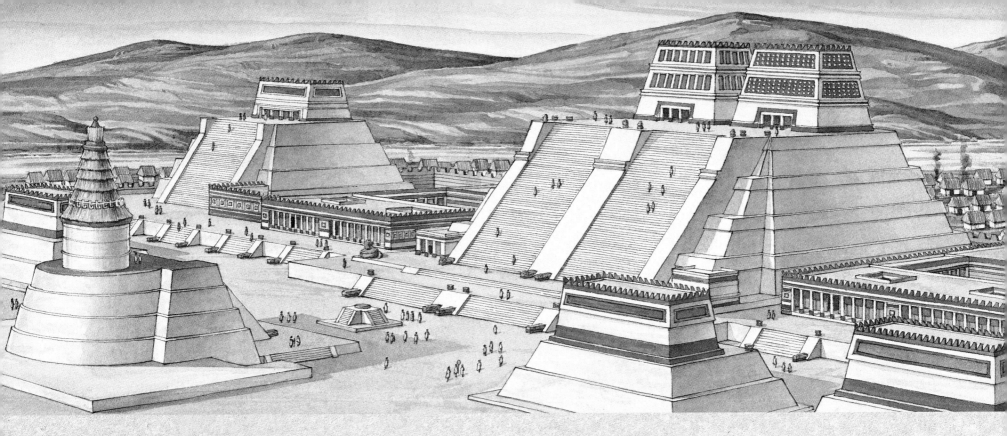

WHY HUMAN SACRIFICE?

For the Aztecs, nothing was more sacred than human sacrifice. They believed that their gods had sacrificed themselves to create the world, and that the best way to pay them back for this sacrifice was by offering them the precious gift of blood. During a sacrifice ceremony four strong priests would hold down the victim while a fifth would plunge a stone knife into his or her chest, wrench out the heart, and then sprinkle blood in the four directions of the compass. Some historians think these sacrifice ceremonies were intended to show people just how powerful the Aztecs were. Whatever the reasons, human sacrifice required a steady stream of victims, most of whom were captured in warfare. This was, in fact, why the Aztecs placed such an emphasis on taking prisoners in battle. They even staged an annual war known as the "flowery war," which had as its sole purpose taking captives. (Left) An Aztec depiction of a sacrifice. (Right) This stone statue, from a very early stage of the temple, held a stone basin into which the

28

hearts of victims were tossed. (Top) A victim's skull found in the ruins of the temple. (Above) Carvings on the skull rack, where the bodies of the sacrificed were displayed.

As the days passed, the Spaniards began to behave more and more strangely. They put Moctezuma under close guard day and night. They scrubbed the blood from the temples and told him there would be no more sacrifices. They said his gods were false, and that his people must worship only the Christian god.

Then they tried to put up a cross and pictures of the Christian saints in the Great Temple.

For once, Moctezuma became angry. He knew now that these Spaniards were not gods or even messengers of Quetzalcoatl. "We have worshipped our own gods here from the beginning," he told Cortés, "and we know they are good. No doubt your god is also good, but we do not want to hear any more about him at present."

He was outraged. These Spaniards were not behaving like guests. They asked Moctezuma where he kept his gold. Then they held his arms and shoulders as he led them to his treasure house. He showed them his prized quetzal feather headdress, his shields, his golden necklaces and armbands.

The Spaniards proceeded to tear all the gold off the shields and jewelry. They melted the gold down into bars and burned the rest, including the feathers that were so precious to the Aztecs. Then they went through all the storage rooms looking for more treasure. They bustled around, poking their noses into everything, arguing among themselves about what to take. They seized all of Moctezuma's precious goods — jewelry made of gold and jade, turquoise crowns, his royal robes. They took it all as if they owned it.

Then they called for fresh food and water. But the people no longer wanted to serve Cortés and his men. They felt as if a fierce beast had invaded their land. Still, they obeyed. They brought food — turkeys, tortillas, eggs, chocolate, fruit —

as well as firewood and fresh water and feed for the Spaniards' animals. They laid everything on the ground with trembling hands and then hurried away as quickly as they could.

May 1520

It was spring, and time for the Feast of Toxcatl. This was the most important festival of the year, in honor of the gods Tezcatlipoca and Huitzilopochtli. The Spaniards told Moctezuma they wanted to see how the festival was celebrated, so preparations began in the Great Temple.

At sundown on the day before the feast, the people began to make a man-sized statue of Huitzilopochtli from seed dough and sticks, as was the tradition. They painted the statue's face and adorned him with turquoise and gold jewels. They gave him a headdress made of hummingbird feathers, a necklace of yellow parrot feathers, wristbands made of coyote skin, a black cape of eagle feathers, and a delicate shield made of reeds.

Dawn broke on the feast day, and the

This mask, created out of a human skull covered in jade, depicts Tezcatlipoca, a god of night, wind, and war.

carefully prepared figure was unveiled. The people placed incense, food, and other gifts before him. Young warriors prepared to sing and dance, proud to show the Spaniards the beautiful rituals of this important feast.

"Come, friends," they called to each other. "Dance with all your hearts!"

The procession began, and the chosen warriors ran into the courtyard to dance. Old men played the drums, and singing echoed off the walls like waves.

Suddenly, in the middle of the dance, the Spaniards closed off the gates to the temple square and ran into the courtyard dressed in their metal armor. They surrounded the dancers and drummers and drew their swords.

"What are you doing, our lords?" the dancers cried. "We are completely unarmed!"

But the Spaniards paid no attention. They smashed the head of Huitzilopochtli. They cut off the arms of one of the drummers. Then they cut off his head, and it rolled across the floor. They attacked all the celebrants, stabbing them with their swords, slashing at their backs and heads.

Some tried to climb the walls to escape. Others pretended to be dead, hoping to save themselves that way, but anyone who stirred was quickly stabbed again.

The blood ran like water, until the floor of the courtyard was slippery with it. The Spaniards killed the women in the palace who were sweeping the floors or grinding corn for their meals. They killed the men who were carrying water to the horses. They ran through the temple, thrusting their swords into every corner in case someone was hidden there.

When the news was heard outside the palace, loud cries rang out. "Bring your shields and spears! The strangers are murdering our warriors!"

The men of Tenochtitlán came at once, almost as if they had been waiting for this moment. They brought their arrows and shields and shot darts at the enemy, until the Spaniards appeared to be covered with yellow reeds.

The Spaniards took refuge in the palace. They

This Aztec drawing shows Moctezuma reading his proclamation — with an armed Spaniard at his back. (Opposite) An Aztec depiction of Cortés's men trapped inside the palace.

fired their guns at the Aztec warriors. And they put Moctezuma in iron chains.

The dead were carried out of the temple. Mothers and fathers wailed with anger and sorrow.

At sunset a proclamation from Moctezuma rang out from the palace roof. He begged his people to abandon the battle for the sake of the children.

But the people were enraged. They fired stones and arrows at the rooftop. Their warriors had been attacked in the middle of a sacred feast. The Spaniards had not sent shields and weapons to them to declare war, as was the Aztec custom. They had been treated as guests in the palace, and then they had turned on their hosts with no warning.

Moctezuma was a coward and a traitor.

Four days later, the Spaniards threw Moctezuma's corpse out of the palace. Some say he had been run through by a Spanish sword. Others say they saw hanging marks around his neck.

Moctezuma's people did not honor him in death. They grumbled that he had been a bad ruler. They put his body on a bed of reeds and set fire to it. The flames blazed up in great tongues, and many said that the body smelled foul as it burned.

The Spaniards stayed in the palace. The people surrounded the building and put guards on all the gates. No one was allowed to take in food or supplies. Then they barricaded the causeways and closed off all the roads to the city.

They would wait for the trapped Spaniards to slowly starve to death.

PART THREE

DEATH OF AN EMPIRE

June 1520

In the dead of night, Cortés and his men crept out of the palace. They moved carefully through the silent city, many of them carrying bars of gold and jewelry that they had stolen.

Luck seemed to be with them. Their steps were muffled by a gentle rain, their movements invisible under the moonless sky. One by one, they crossed the canals using a wooden bridge they had made. But at the fourth canal, they came upon a woman fetching water. She knew right away who they were.

"Come quickly!" she screamed. "Our enemies are escaping!"

The Aztec warriors wasted no time. Some came running down the causeway. Others leaped into their boats and paddled so furiously that it looked as if the water were boiling. They surrounded the fleeing enemy. Many Spaniards threw themselves headfirst into the water, scattering the gold as they jumped.

The battle lasted all night. Slowly, Cortés's men fought their way out of Moctezuma's city. One canal was so full of dead men and horses that the Spaniards who followed were able to cross the canal by stepping on the bodies.

At dawn the Aztecs cleared the dead out of the canals and threw them into the reedy part of the lake. Then they searched the bottoms of the canals to gather up the stolen gold, along with everything else the Spaniards had left behind — their swords, steel helmets, shields, and armor.

All summer long the Aztecs celebrated their victory with feasts and festivals, just as they had always done. They repaired and decorated the temple. They reopened the market, swept the streets, and put their houses back in order.

Cortés and the Spaniards were gone. The people of Tenochtitlán told themselves that now life could return to normal.

September 1520

It was the middle of August when people began to feel sick. They shivered with cold, even in the blazing heat. Children complained of aches in their backs and limbs. Many took to their beds in the middle of the day, hoping that the darkness indoors might ease their terrible headaches. People could be seen retching in the streets or bent over with pain and dizziness.

Then the spots appeared. Raised red sores grew for two weeks and eventually bubbled up in blisters. They appeared on the arms and face, then spread down the body over the stomach, the back, and the legs.

No one had seen an illness like this before. In a city so big and so crowded, it was impossible to isolate the sick. The disease was carried swiftly through Tenochtitlán on every breath and with every touch.

For some, the pain was so great that they couldn't even move on their sleeping mats without crying out. Many starved to death because they could not get up to fetch food. Few were left to look after the sick or tend the fields. When there were too many bodies to burn or bury, they were paddled out into the middle of the lake and dumped, or rolled into the canals.

Death took many. For others, the fever passed, and the blisters dried up. But when the scabs fell off, they left dark brown marks and pits that stayed on the victim's face like a death mask. Some were blinded for life.

After two months the plague moved through Tenochtitlán and spread to all the neighboring lands. The survivors sighed with relief. Surely the gods' anger was exhausted now. Surely the days of death were over for good.

WHY DID EVERYONE GET SICK?

Smallpox, the disease that hit the Aztecs, was quite common in the Old World. But in Spain, most people would have developed some resistance to it. They might get sick but few people would die. The Aztecs had no such resistance. When the Spaniards brought the disease into their world, they died in the tens of thousands.

May 1521

Word spread quickly through Tenochtitlán. Cortés and his soldiers were returning. They had gathered together an army in Tlaxcala. With supplies brought from the coast and the help of native allies, they were quickly building brigantines on the other side of the lake.

This time the people heard not only the sound of horses' hooves pounding the causeways, but trumpets and drums and gunfire announcing the attack. Most terrifying of all were the screams and shouts of the Tlaxcalans. There were thousands upon thousands of them. They sang war songs as they came, stirring up a cloud of dust so great that their bodies and faces looked gray. The Aztecs' old enemies swarmed through the city, hungry to take revenge for all the defeats they had suffered in the past.

When the Spaniards returned, they had boats equipped with cannons that could bombard the city.

The people of Tenochtitlán tried to put barriers on the causeways. But they could not stop the Spanish ships, which anchored nearby and pointed their cannons at the island city.

The Aztec warriors leaped into canoes and paddled out to attack the Spaniards. But their tiny boats, carved from tree trunks, were no match for the big ships.

Cortés's men fired at the city with their guns. They tore down houses and threw the bricks and beams into the canals so their horses could ride through the streets more easily. The Aztecs fought bravely, but even their deadly *macanas* were no match for the Spanish crossbows, guns, cannons, and catapults.

Finally many decided to flee. Some bundled their children into canoes and paddled away in panic, leaving

*This painting shows the final moments of the Aztec empire. Here Spanish soldiers
capture Cuauhtémoc, the last emperor of the Aztecs. His capture marked the end of the struggle.
(Opposite) For the once-proud Aztecs, conquest meant total obedience to Spanish rule.*

all their belongings behind. Others crowded the causeways leading to the mainland, carrying their children on their shoulders. Some of the children laughed, thinking it was great fun to ride on their parents this way. It made them as tall as the men in iron helmets who rode the tame deer.

But others wailed and cried. The air was black with gunsmoke. It darkened the sky like night. Families became separated. Fathers, mothers, and children cried as they searched for each other in the darkness.

The battle wore on, through days and weeks. The Spaniards broke the aqueduct that brought fresh water to the city. The lake water and canals became polluted with the bodies of the dead. Some people drank it anyway and became sick.

There was no food in the city. People ate lizards, swallows, straw, weeds and wood. They ate dirt and chewed old pieces of deer hide.

Then the Spaniards brought out their biggest cannon and took it to the Great Temple. They placed it on the sacred sacrificial stone. The temple priests beat their drums, calling the warriors of the city to come and defend the shrine. But the Spanish soldiers cut down the priests with their swords and threw them down the steps.

After eighty days, the Spaniards claimed victory. They rode through the city and set the temples on fire. They searched every building and every body — dead and living — looking for gold. They fed some of their captives to their dogs. They took the strongest young Aztec men for slaves, branding their cheeks or lips with hot irons.

When it was all over, Moctezuma's magnificent birds had been burned in their cages, homes had been plundered, and the streets were littered with rotting bodies.

And the unlucky people who remained looked at the ruins of their once-great city and wept.

EPILOGUE

When the siege of Tenochtitlán was over, nearly half a million lives had been lost. Almost all of the dead were native people, both Aztecs and allies of Cortés. Many more died from illness, lack of food, and polluted water than in battle. And long after Tenochtitlán fell, its people continued to die of diseases that had been brought to the New World by Europeans.

By the time the Aztecs surrendered to the Spanish, only 30,000 people remained in Tenochtitlán. By 1600, the population of Mexico was one-quarter what it had been under Moctezuma. And the city that Cortés had himself described as the most beautiful in the world lay in ruins.

The Spaniards destroyed what they could of the

Great Temple, blowing it up with several hundred barrels of gunpowder. Then they built Christian churches on top of the rubble and transformed Tenochtitlán into the Spanish settlement that eventually became Mexico City. European settlers came to manage the land, and many Aztecs ended up working as farmers or miners for their new bosses. Children were baptized and given Spanish names and sent to Spanish schools.

The Europeans brought horses and animals for food to their new settlements. The rats and cockroaches that stowed away on their ships thrived in the Americas, which had never seen such creatures. But the sheep, cattle, and goats overgrazed the land and polluted the canals. Eventually the shallow lake surrounding Tenochtitlán was drained.

Today, much of the base of the Great Temple (above) in central Mexico City has been unearthed. (Opposite) These stone figures were uncovered during excavation. (Left top) A similar pyramid that has been restored gives some idea of what the Great Temple would have looked like. (Bottom left) Remnants of the Great Temple's skull rack, where the remains of sacrificial victims were put on display.

43

Today Mexico's presidential palace stands on top of what was once Moctezuma's home, which Cortés had said was grander than any king's castle in Europe. A modern road has been built over the causeway that once carried the Spaniards into Tenochtitlán. And the bustling marketplace that the Europeans so admired is now a railway yard and slums.

After the giant moon goddess stone was discovered in Mexico City in 1978, archaeologist Eduardo Matos Moctezuma and his team spent five

(Opposite) Two archaeologists carefully work on a human skeleton discovered in the ruins. Among other items found were (left) a statue depicting Quetzalcoatl as an Aztec merchant (right) a funeral urn, (far right, top) a mask showing the god Xipe Totec and (far right, bottom) the blade from a sacrifical knife.

years excavating the Great Temple. They found more than seven thousand artifacts. There were finely carved jade masks and statues, jewelry made of gold, silver, and turquoise, musical instruments, razor-sharp weapons and tools, rooms full of shells and coral, and many human and animal remains. No one knows what other treasures may still lie buried there.

(Top) Now open to the public, the Great Temple produced thousands of fascinating objects, such as (bottom left) this skull pierced by a stone knife and (bottom right) a carved detail of the pyramid.

The archaeologists quickly saw that the Great Temple was the center of a remarkable civilization. The Aztecs were skilled architects, builders, traders, musicians, and poets. They lived in well-run, comfortable, clean cities. They were careful tenders of the soil, able to grow an astonishing variety of food plants to feed huge populations without using beasts of burden, the wheel, or iron tools. They also practiced harsh and bloody rituals to show their devotion to their gods and their communities. They saw human beings as just one part of nature, with a duty to maintain the cycles of the natural world.

Most of all they were a powerful state of warriors who met their match when a small but determined force of strangers appeared in their land one day. The Aztecs welcomed the visitors and led them into their city. They housed them, fed them, gave them their most precious treasures, and showed them their sacred feasts and rituals.

They didn't realize that the Spaniards were warriors like themselves who had come to the New World to gain riches and glory for their country and their church. Their mission was successful. But for the Aztecs the Spanish victory meant much more than defeat in war. It meant the loss of their entire civilization.

GLOSSARY

aqueduct: A long bridge, designed to carry water. An aqueduct carried water across Lake Texcoco to Tenochtitlán.

archaeologist: A person who studies people from the past and their cultures.

artifact: Any historical object created by humans.

brigantine: A small sailing ship with two masts.

causeway: A raised road that crosses water or low land.

Chalchiuhtlicue: (chal-chee-oot-li-cue) Female deity who watched over lakes, rivers, and the ocean.

Coyolxauhqui: (coy-oll-zah-kee) Moon goddess.

excavating/excavate: To dig up artifacts or a skeleton or even an entire city or temple that has been long buried.

Huitzilopochtli: (het-sil-o-pock-tlee) Aztec god of war.

incense: A substance that gives off a pleasant smell when burned.

macana: A wooden club fitted with sharp cutting blades made of obsidian.

Nahuatl: (na-watt-ull) The language the Aztecs spoke. It is still spoken in some parts of Mexico.

obsidian: A volcanic rock that resembles black glass. Can be made very sharp.

proclamation: An official order or command, often made by a king to his subjects

prophecy: A statement about what will happen in the future.

quetzal: (ket-zahl) A colorful bird native to Mexico.

Quetzalcoatl: (ket-zahl-coat-ull) Aztec god whose name meant "feathered serpent."

sacrifice: An offering of something precious (in the Aztecs' case, often a human life) to a god or gods.

shrine: A building where prayer and worship are offered to a god or gods.

Tenochtitlán: (te-noch-ti-tlan) Capital city of the Aztec empire.

Tezcatlipoca: (tez-cat-lah-poca) Aztec god whose name meant "smoking mirror."

tlatoani: (til-at-oh-ani) A Nahuatl word meaning speaker, it was the title given to Moctezuma. It is typically translated to mean "emperor."

tribute: A payment made by one nation or king to another.

zocalo: The main square at the heart of modern-day Mexico City.

RECOMMENDED FURTHER READING

Aztec, Inca and Maya
by Elizabeth Baquenado (Knopf)
An illustrated book that looks at the three great pre-Columbian civilizations of the Americas — the Aztecs and Mayas of Mexico and the Incas of Peru.

Aztecs
by Fiona MacDonald (Barron's Educational Series)
Hundreds of photographs and pictures bring the civilization of the fabulous Aztec kingdom to life.

How Would You Survive as an Aztec?
by Fiona MacDonald (Franklin Watts)
A look at everyday life in the Aztec world, that brings it alive for modern readers by asking such questions as "What would I eat and drink?"

The Aztec News
Phillip Steele, ed. (Candlewick Press)
Using the format of a daily newspaper, this book looks at life in the Aztec empire and recounts the growth of Aztec power and the Spanish conquest.

PICTURE CREDITS

All illustrations are by Greg Ruhl unless otherwise stated. Every effort has been made to attribute correctly all material reproduced in this book. If any errors have unwittingly occurred, we will be happy to correct them in future editions.

Front cover: (Upper left) Spanish School. *Capture of Guatemoc.* British Embassy, Mexico City, courtesy of Bridgeman Art Library International Inc.(Upper right) British Museum, London. Werner Forman Archive, courtesy of Bridgeman Art Library International Ltd. (Lower left) George Holton, Photo Researchers, Inc. (Lower right) Andrew Rakoczy, Photo Researchers, Inc.

Back cover: (Middle) *The City of Tenochtitlan* by Miguel Cvarrubias, Museo Nacional de Antropologia, Mexico City, D.F., Courtesy of Shwalkijk/ Art Resource. (Right) Pigorini Museum of Prehistory and Ethnography, Rome. Werner Forman Archive, courtesy of Art Resource

1: Courtesy of Art Resource
4: David Hiser, Photographers/Aspen
5: (All) Andrew Rakoczy, Photo Researchers, Inc.
6: *The City of Tenochtitlan*
7: Diagram by Jack McMaster
9: Biblioteca Medicea-Laurenziana, Florence, courtesy of Bridgeman Art Library International Ltd.
10: Maps by Jack McMaster (Bottom left) Instituto Nacional de Antropologia e Historia, Mexico, D.F.

11: (Left) George Holton, Photo Researchers Inc. (Right) Courtesy of Bridgeman Art Library International Ltd.
12: British Museum, London. Werner Forman Archive, courtesy of Art Resource
14: Biblioteca Nazionale Centrale, Florence, courtesy of the Bridgeman Art Library International Inc.
15: (Left) Pigorini Museum of Prehistory and Ethnography, Rome. Werner Forman Archive, courtesy of Art Resource. (Bottom) Private collection, courtesy of Bridgeman Art Library International Ltd.
16: (Left) Art Resource (Right) North Wind Picture Archive
18: Diagram by Jack McMaster
19: (Left) Museum fur Volkerkunde, Vienna. Photo by Erich Lessing, courtesy of Art Resource (Right) Diagram by Jack McMaster
24: (Top) J.P. Courau, DDB Stock Photography (Bottom) David Ryan, DDB Stock Photography
26: D. Donne Bryant, DDB Stock Photography
27: D. Donne Bryant, DDB Stock Photography
28: (Top) Diagram by Jack McMaster (Bottom) Biblioteca Nazionale, Florence, courtesy of Art Resource
28-29: Instituto Nacional de Antropologia e Historia, Mexico, D.F.
29: (Top) David Hiser, Photographers/Aspen (Bottom) D. Donne Bryant, DDB Stock Photography

30: British Museum, London. Werner Forman Archive, courtesy of Art Resource
32: D. Donne Bryant, DDB Stock Photography
33: Biblioteca Nacional, Madrid, Spain, courtesy of Bridgeman Art Library International Ltd.
38: D. Donne Bryant, DDB Stock Photography
40: Spanish School. *Capture of Guatemoc.* British Embassy. Mexico City, courtesy of Bridgeman Art Library International Ltd.
41: D. Donne Bryant, DDB Stock Photography
42: David Hiser, Photographers/Aspen
43: (Top) George Chan, Photo Researchers Inc. (Middle) J.P. Courau, DDB Stock Photography (Bottom) D. Donne Bryant, DDB Stock Photography
44: David Hiser, Photographers/Aspen
45: (Left) St. Louis Art Museum, courtesy of Art Resource (Right) D. Donne Bryant, DDB Stock Photography (Top right) British Museum, London. Courtesy of Bridgeman Art Library International Ltd. (Bottom right) David Hiser, Photographers/Aspen
46: (Top) Andrew Rakoczy, Photo Researchers, Inc. (Bottom left) David Hiser, Photographers/ Aspen (Bottom right) David Hiser, Photographers/Aspen
48: British Museum, London. Werner Forman Archive, courtesy of Art Resource

ACKNOWLEDGMENTS

The text of this book is largely based on Aztec accounts taken from a number of sources, including *We People Here: Nahuatl Accounts of the Conquest of Mexico* (edited by James Lockhart); *The Broken Spears: The Aztec Account of the Conquest of Mexico* (edited by Miguel Leon-Portilla); and Book 12 of the *Florentine Codex: General History of the Things of New Spain* by Bernardino de Sahagún.

Madison Press would like to thank the following: our principal adviser, Dr. Eduardo Matos Moctezuma, director of the Museo del Templo Mayor in Mexico City; and Alba Agosto, for her translation work.

Design and Art Direction: Gordon Sibley Design Inc.

Maps and Diagrams: Jack McMaster

Editorial Director: Hugh M. Brewster

Project Editor: Ian R. Coutts

Editorial Assistance: Susan Aihoshi, Nan Froman

Production Director: Susan Barrable

Production Co-ordinator: Donna Chong

Color Separation: Colour Technologies

Printing and Binding: Tien Wah Press, Singapore

Lost Temple of the Aztecs was produced by Madison Press Books, which is under the direction of Albert E. Cummings